D1446912

THIS HOLDING ON,
THIS LETTING GO

New and Selected
Poems by
Karen Updike

Fireweed Press
P.O. Box 482
Madison, WI 53701-0482

Printed by Inkwell Printers, LLC
Dodgeville, Wisconsin
www.inkwellprinters.com

For my sister,
Kirsten Lokvam Chapman
who has always been encouraging
and shared with me the pleasure of writing

Acknowledgments

I want to thank our longstanding and supportive Wednesday afternoon manuscript group, my Fireweed editors, Jeri McCormick and Robin Chapman, my landscape artist friend Leslie DeMuth and the Chazen Museum of Art at the University of Wisconsin, formerly the Elvehjem Museum, whose works of art provided inspiration for many of the poems in this book.

Some of these poems were previously printed in calendars published by The Wisconsin Fellowship of Poets, and in Wisconsin Poets at the Elvehjem Museum of Art, The Madison Review and Sonja, published by E. J. Hill in 1981.

Cover art: Mother and Child by William Zorach
Cover photo by Karen Updike

Author's photo by Jean Duesler

OF ART AND ME

WAITING FOR LANGUAGE

IN MY TIME

CULTIVATING BLUEBIRDS

OF ART AND ME

I Could Have Been In Pictures

You know that alienated effect they were always after,
Edward Hopper and Andrew Wyeth?
They should have painted me at fifteen

loitering on a pass from study hall
near a narrow window in the girls' bathroom
overlooking Lake Michigan,

my arms forming a triangle against the sill
while fifty yards beyond and two stories below
waves gnawed the crumbling breakwater.

Hopper would have painted me from a passing freighter,
mine the one face in that row of uniform windows
along the old Milwaukee yellow brick wall,

some shades up, or half way up
some curtains drawn, or partially drawn,
row upon row of eyeless dormitory rooms.

Wyeth would have painted the window from the inside,
as he did the one in Ground Hog Day,
but there I would be again, painted this time from the back,

just me gazing at that yacht sailing out there
where the Sisters said, in the year before the lake rose,
they had picked apples and built bonfires.

He would paint it in winter, show beyond it
the mountains of ice the lake spewed up with each wave,
how the spray frosted parts of the pane even that high up

so that I could take my gold cross off its chain,
grasp it like a tool, and etch designs in the ice --
somehow manage to make my mark.

On The Dubious Merit Of Ignoring The Visible

"Those people are always more pleasing to God
who have sought what is essential in the invisible
and ignored the visible as non-essential."

Robertson Davies

Of course the invisible is less messy
and far less embarrassing.
It need not be cleaned up
or covered up
and one can always imagine it
as better than in fact it is.
The visible, on the other hand,
say a flower, or a landscape,
does draw the senses.
A face may at times
make one forget
the supremacy of the invisible altogether.
When that occurs
it must be dealt with:
Religion, or hard work,
may suffice.
Consider running for public office.
Get on a board of directors
and work for someone else's
good cause.
If the visible persists
in penetrating,
avoid poetry, dance concerts,
art galleries and arboretums.
Never, never
plant a garden.

The Violinist At His Loom

Music is a fluid art

When a violinist sits down at a loom
it must be because he is so obsessed
with strings, any strings, that he must
draw something across them,
a bow, a shuttle, something that fills up space
with slim threads of melody or meaning.

All the long afternoon he plays his loom
with the warp through the heddles
his feet dancing the treadles
as he separates the shed,
plies his shuttle across the threads
all the long afternoon playing his loom
changing accent and tempo
making rhythms flow
not with sound but with color.

Following several hours at his loom
in the sunlit room it must be gratifying to find
that the piece he has woven is stunning,
though silent, and what is more, it lasts.

Living With Art

written about the Sirac Collection in Columbus, Ohio

Imagine tidying up after such a dinner party,
having to realign the Rodin some guest left rotated
toward the garden, his glance skimming the courtyard.
Think of straightening frames that hold Monets,
wiping finger prints from bronzes she told us
we could touch because "This is not a museum."
Imagine replacing the hall vase daily with flowers fresh
as the Van Dougan lilacs rising behind them, or trying
to find a space large enough for your new Jawlensky.
Think of needing, all these years, only two lamps
in the vast living room, so much light flooded
from above the paintings.
Then, when going out for the evening,
think of always turning on the one
above the smaller Degas for your night light.

Earthquake Madonna

Even as we view her, over coffee and scones,
upper front page of our New York Times,
she gazes out at us from a makeshift tent
high in a Himalayan hamlet, ninety thousand
countrymen around or beneath her
dead in the rubble of their ravaged homes.

Praise the photographer who immortalized her,
the editors who featured her.
Praise the institutions they attended,
the art professors who taught them.
Praise the old masters, Rembrandt, Caravaggio,
who influence still our seeing and composing,
or how would comfortable millions
be drawn out of their security to empathize
with victims of yet another natural disaster
from the other side of the world?

There's smoke from her fire in the foreground,
she is warm enough today, and plastic tarps crumpled
but rising in the shadow of some higher structure.
Freshly lashed poles hold the whole thing together,
at least until winter, and heavy rumpled blankets
tumble a woven nest, showing flashes
of orange, green and black, like her country's flag.

And then, centered, we find the Madonna,
vulnerable in her thin wool scarf, with her child,
his yellow knit cap and rust colored snow suit.
She's lifting him under the arms the way I did my toddlers,
and of course he avoids the photographer
who is holding something black, like an elephant trunk.
The mother eyes the stranger sternly, with resignation.
He is intruding, but these days, so much has.
And then I would imagine, she turns her attention back,
back to the bigger problem, keeping her son warm.

The Bronze Before The Elvehjem Museum Door

She will be forever young, this bronze,
her babe ever straddling her knee.
Fast-growing locusts planted here
will shield them needlessly.

Though snowdust shawls her shoulders
or greys the part in her hair,
this mother and child memorial
embodies an eternal pair.

But when I pass this Madonna
my emotional barometer reads low,
for even on 'up' days it seems to me
her child is struggling to go.

Not passively on display
like madonnas and babes within,
this boy seems somewhat contentious;
would he turn his back on kin?

He faces west expectantly,
she commerce and mid-town.
her massive arms support him;
she will never let him down.

She makes of herself a ladder,
he climbs to upright stance,
but his forearms separate their hearts,
he casts a distant glance.

This mother and son seem at odds,
as if they want different things.
Do her eyes foreshadow the terrible pain
her need to control him will bring?

Unlike this woman, I will age.
In my heart understanding can grow.
Since my arms are not cast in bronze,
may they learn now how to let go.

*Originally this statue by William Zorach was on a high pedestal
facing University Avenue in Madison, Wisconsin*

On "Wounded"

a painting by Sundt-Hanson

Sitting near her husband's sick bed,
her child wrapped in a shawl
the same weave
as her head scarf,
oh she is weary,
she is not up to this much
being demanded of her,
and nowhere to turn.
She was meant for more.
Even his death
would have been easier.

Wounded, Who Knows How

Yes, wounded,
who knows how,
or cares, for that matter?

Don't you suppose
others are also hurt,
those whose blood

may not seep
through bandages,
whose pain is private

and rarely painted,
but just as real,
even in repercussion?

In Gallery V at the Elvehjem Museum

Except for the family portrait of Lady Torrence
this is a quiet gallery of unaffected people.

The plowman waters his team
savoring pastel light.

The cowherd wends her way
welcoming the shade.

Packhorses lie down
for their noonday rest.

The lion family relaxes
content and well fed.

Two visiting friends share
an unmarked moment to laugh.

a woman in a green hat
retires for a moment into herself.

as does the young girl
who resorts to a cool arbor

and a child basks in the gaze
of the friend who took her apple picking.

But you may be sure no matter how soon
Lady Torrence's brood tires of their lavish

picture books and spinning tops,
their painting lessons and silly pranks on nurse,

they will never be allowed to linger
on the river bank with other picnickers

or hear the fishermen's tales at Etretat
as they mend nets and clean traps.

They will never pat the farmer's dog,
pick apples with the cotter's child,

or walk barefoot into a misty landscape.
Their outing to see the lions at the animal park

might have to be postponed innumerable times
for all sorts of good reasons.

They might be encouraged instead to visit
Worcester's gloomy nave, or finish their Virgil.

Perhaps on a sunny day like today,
a stroll around their grounds would be nice.

Whatever they do, they must keep their cuffs clean,
for she has scheduled another sitting at two.

On "After The Fight"

a painting by Sundt-Hanson

Even his fiddle was bashed in the brawl.
Anyone can tell he is still fuming.
He grasps his bandaged hand
as if it were his enemy.
A passionate fellow, he wears silver beads
around his neck. Perhaps he sings as well.
Whatever he does or did not do
he cannot be hurting as much as these two
who have traveled all this way in search of him,
leaving behind farm and fjord
for the city, where they fear he wastes
his days in sleep, his nights in revelry.
Now mother and sister stand before him
on his unswept floor.

What artist could not paint the disappointment
the son sees sagging on his mother's face?
From us it is averted; only two folds of skin
to the left of her chin show how long
with disapproval it really is.
She has tried to make a Christian of him.
But he has been a hard one to mold,
always kicking over the traces,
climbing the tallest trees,
as if trying to prove something,
the kind that goes looking for trouble
and, expecting the worst, finds it.
Where he got that from, she will never guess.

His sister can scarcely sort out her tears.
She cries for them all, her brother so rash,
her mother so harsh and hard to please,
herself so helpless to intervene.
No matter how good and obedient
she tries to be, he ruins it all.
Knowing how harshly mama berates herself
for all their mistakes does not stop him.
She can't bear to see mamma like this.
To make up for Johan, she will have to be
better than ever.

On "Grandmother's Bridal Crown"
a painting by Adolph Tidemand, 1869

After the mid-day meal, the bread and cheese
back in the corner cupboard,
long hours ahead, and no cloth on her loom,
whose idea was it to open the trunk
that bright afternoon
when surely there were goats to chase,
and new kittens in the mow?

Did the children beg to see her bridal crown?
Or did the grandmother herself,
seeing how the skin of the oldest child
shone like milk in a pail,
and remembering another child's
long blond hair, did the old woman
herself suggest opening it,
that they might stay inside with her?

With the smallest key at her belt
she turned the lock, releasing
leather hinges in the domed chest,
wafting musty air into cottage light.
She came first upon her wedding vest
and dowry belt, then reached farther
down to what was wrapped in paper
all crumpled from many viewings –

and sitting there beneath the shutters
where the light is good, she hears
the children gasp as paper and time fall away.
There, gold as was her Anna's hair, they see
the eight point crown, a tiny cross atop each spire
gleaming before them like the grail.

But as she holds the crown out to them,
her own eyes, glowing like old pewter,
seek only her granddaughter's frail face.

23

On "Portrait of Mrs. Pearce"

a painting by Charles Pearce

You are indeed beautiful, Mrs. Pearce
and richly deserve that plumy hat
which quite sets off your coal black hair.
And oh! The silver head
of your be-ribboned walking stick!
It must be the latest sensation.
I hate to think what beguiling things
you manage with that gorgeous shawl,
pure sacrilege, of course, to cover
shoulders snowy as yours.

Now I don't know whether you wanted to pose,
or anything else, for your husband that day,
but I do call your attention to the thistles
he chose to include in your portrait,
not pansies or roses, but thistles, Mrs. Pearce,
and quite frankly, I counsel you to look at your manners,
lest you provoke him further, for it does seem to me,
and I may be mistaken, that he has painted the darkness
of your bonnet's chinstrap more severely,
yes, indeed, rather more severely,
than any satisfied man would deem necessary.

Albert Bierstadt Sketches What Is To Become The Boating Party

Yesterday he painted from the eagle's nest,
noting how light changed the dells' rocky face,
discovering steely glints in water below.
Today he will try again, this time from the canoe,
how best to convey their majesty, and his awe.

The current pulls him past cliff walls
where lichen lines niches, where rocks bind
roots of grotesquely cantilevered trees,
where blue bells cling amidst tufted grasses
and he thinks, as he opens his notebook,

yes, this vantage point far surpasses the heights,
when a boating party comes into view
around the next bluff, a fragile splintery bark
no larger, from where he drifts, than a grasshopper.
Canvas furled, they are anchored for swimming.

Flipping to a clean page, he roughs in the harsh profile
of the next bluff, and the hazy mountain beyond,
notes the pronounced line of demarcation
between green shaded water and lazy blue-pink air,
sketches their boat swiftly, drifting closer as he draws,

so that he sees a woman sharply retract her left leg,
the water shrill where the dells are deep,
then writes down and underlines the word yellow
to remind himself, when he paints this cavernous cool,
how sunlight illuminated the lichen.

On "Portrait of Michael Tapie"

a sculpture by Alexander Calder, 1930

Calder must have started his portrait
in the middle of the immeasurably long piece of wire,
doubling it to form
the bridge of Tapie's nose
and then, in mirror image,
all the soft tissue parts
twisting the wire
with considerable torque
to form the elongated nostrils,
his spiral eyes, his delicate ears.
In defining his jawbone and brow,
he conjured Tapie's entire skull
out of thin air
and fastened the sculpture to its base
with his own wire signature.

The question nevertheless remains:
Why did Calder render him in wire?
A modest unassuming man,
Tapie seems to age
from the youthful jester
revealed in the frontal view
to the man of substance
depicted in the left profile,
(the sort of man through whom
one could never see).
And finally, when the quiescence of old age,
represented by the right profile, caught up with him,
he was hardly one of whom it could have been said,
"Michael, you're really wired!"

On "Still Life With Watermelon"

a painting by Severin Roesen

Even before Roesen painted this still life, someone,
perhaps Roesen himself, had made the centerpiece a work of art,
tumbling strawberries like garnets from that carefully tipped basket,
placing the wine glass precisely, and snipping those grapes
slyly on a slant from the vine, then clustering them with cherries
among larger fruited globes.

But it was his brush which made
the velvet-skinned peaches glow like setting suns,
the leathery orange rinds gleam like fish scales.
It was his brush that dusted the purple plums
and smoothed the nectarines, it was his brush
that glistened the lemon slices
and dotted those watermelon seeds randomly
into their crevices. It was his brush, you must believe me,
which wound that escaping tendril of grapevine
into his signature, and munched those holes
in that otherwise perfect leaf.

I Talked To A Weaver

I talked to an artist about weaving my hills.
Could color and pattern evoke earth and sky?
I hoped the piece would evoke what I saw
after riding up out of the valley, turning back
and seeing hills, green and gold for the gazing
field by field sloping away to left and right
like jagged lightning patterns on Navaho blankets
and dark as thunderheads, background ridges
of hickory and oak scudded against the sky.

I knew she wove her own fibers,
made her own dyes. I wanted each color
to recall the woods and fields I rode,
the texture depict their bristling brush,
padded contours, rock outcroppings.
I asked if she could weave in pebbles and bark,
fray coarse twine, crumble twigs
to suggest the crackling underbrush.

When we got around to talking price, she quoted
a figure per square inch farmers would not pay
if they had to buy acres that way. But I believed
her weaving would be so true it would help
those who had not loved the land to revere it,
and those who have, to remember.

Wherever Water

Over the stone wall
only the tops of fruit trees,

graduated, so I know
there must be terraces,

and yes, formal gardens
and fountains, and oh,

pathways, drawing the eye
down to water, always to water.

Wherever I am, Lake Champlain,
cub beach or the cove,

wherever downcast eyes
pause to recreate, they choose,

don't they? the heights,
and water, water to gaze over,

water to catch the message
of the wind, water,

with its perpetual painting
of the sky.

WAITING FOR LANGUAGE

Waiting For Language

The silence of animals and the silence of nature
would not be so great and noble if it were
merely a failure of language to materialize.

Max Picard, The World of Silence

This will be a writing morning,
no television news, no coffee,
no frosty newspaper retrieved from the porch.
In lowered metabolic state the dog snoozes on,
while under the pillow the phone bleats and is still,
and I am disconnected from a world where a father
might be breathing his last, where children
in distress might be signaling for help,
and as remote in this contrived silence
as I am in the slow snowfall of a deep woods,
I crouch over my tablet,
waiting for language.

Poetry Scrabble

If I could write poems with friends
as easily as I play Scrabble with them,
tea and snacks close at hand,
the conflictual world kept at bay,
I would have whole sheaves to read!

In turn we'd reach into our soft sack
of memories, pull out images and quotes,
assemble them deftly into meanings
heretofore unrecognized, unknown,
until all assembled, beheld: a poem!

Awaiting each other's production,
friends might reach for mixed nuts,
offer jolting insights, or humorous remarks
to lighten the poet's task, enabling each
to finish before time was up.

Then at evening's end, instead of ruefully
funneling small tiles back into the bag,
disrupting our intricately assembled
but intrinsically meaningless word maker,
we would have the exquisite pleasure

of taking home one poem,
etched in our hearts,
or even on paper!

On Reading May Sarton

(for a book group who thought I would like to review her)

It is true, I am a woman who likes poetry, friends and flowers
but I assure you, I am growing more tired than the author
of her perpetual parade of visitors, their soulful walks together

overlooking the sea, their picnics out, their interminable dinners in,
such a grievous burden it must have been, fixing all those lobsters,
popping all those corks, arranging all those bouquets.

I am sure her friends never tire of hearing how bogged down she is
by her vast personal correspondence, her immense garden.
Although some may find it far from flattering to read how
        relieved she was

after they finally left, to get back to what she considers
her solitary "real self," others take pity on the old girl,
pitch right in, raking her leaves, cleaning out her files,

even arranging readings and book signings, transportation and lodgings
(in well-placed homes with compliant cats and exquisite views
of another part of the sea).

But I would like to say to her, "Stop your belly-aching!
Cull your correspondence as you do the weeds in your garden.
And for God's sake, quit ordering bulbs!"

And Me Without My Camera

When I saw a father and young son
emerging from the café,
necks draped with binoculars and cameras,

I rushed over on winged heels
staying their departure with my upraised hand,
my intense stare:

"Vines," I cried, "There's Boston ivy
just up Walnut Drive on those concrete bulwarks.
Young vines, barely leafed out. They're etching
retaining walls, their patterns diffuse as veins,
as expressive as art. And in this early light,
they reveal their redness, their fine designs.
You could photograph them, don't you see?
They won't look like that for long."

"Well, we're out for birds today, not vines,"
they smiled, pulling away.
"Why don't you take your own pictures?"

The Poet Holds A Garage Sale

Mad for more space and craving new order
I decide to plan a garage sale as my neighbor did.
Since Goodwill rejected her broken appliances
and children's games, it is sure to refuse my poems
with missing parts. To the trash I drag all work lacking
central metaphors, all derivative poems
and poems which try to be funny but fail.

Down in the storeroom I sort crates overflowing
with poems. This one is old-fashioned and rhymes,
but someone might enjoy it.
This has a chipped spout, but still pours.
I never did like that one's shape
and I've quite outgrown this view.
This is merely thought untextured by image.
That could only have been published at the time.
One exposes an appalling self pity,
another mistakes emotion for uniqueness.
I have lost the cord to this,
the insides to that, one is limed up,
another badly stained.
Here's still another poem about trail riding,
my over-used image of escape.

Out in the garage late at night, too late
to ask my neighbor's advice,
I group and price them;
starts of poems in an old clothes hamper:
two for fifty cents.
Poems with expired shelf lives in a cracked crock:
ten cents a piece.
Jumbles of images draped like fabric remnants
on the garden fence,
two for a quarter.

But this one, about driving away
from the farm that last time,
the harvest moon punctuating two slopes
like an immense period,
this might be worth keeping.
I slip it into my pocket for later.

On the craft table, instead of patterns,
macramé beads and candle molds,
I spread my first attempts
at sonnets, sestinas, villanelles,
then designate one sturdy box
for books on how to write,
another for marketing strategies,
a third for chapbooks
by angry women I no longer read.

Downstairs again, I drape ghostly sheets
over poems I cannot bear to discard.
I would like to browse, but it's late,
I still have so much to do,
the cash box to seed, coffee to prepare,
signs to make for Midvale and Mohawk.
I pry open an old paint can, brown like our house,
print wearily, with a wide brush:

GARAGE SALE TODAY!
POETRY!
ONE TIME ONLY!

Stuff And Nonsense

"What is more trying than other people's memories,
unless it is other people's dreams?"

Amanda Cross in *The Theban Mysteries*

Clearly she is not speaking about poets.
When Elizabeth Bishop freed her tremendous fish,
that became quite a memory.
When Coleridge woke up from Kubla Khan
he knew that had been quite an experience.
When I dreamed I was the perfect hostess
I decided that was some kind of a warning.

You see, a family of burglars, a father
and his two daughters, came to loot my house
and for some reason I simply let them stay
until they went away.

We're still apprentices, the girls explained,
but if we hold up, dad says he'll help us
join a really good gang.

So much they wanted was bolted down,
their work was slow, but the father wielded
an acetylene torch and wore a welder's shield
round as an ophthalmologist's mirror.
I admired his skill and told him so,
found black trash bags for their loot,
and hovered about forever, hoping
they would feel right at home.

Of course the burglar alarm kept ringing
but I hastened to reassure them time
and time again. "Oh it always acts like that,"
I would say, and just kept turning it,
just kept turning it off.

It's Not Much, But

there remains some solace
in writing by hand

on paper you choose
and the pen you use –

Scratch! Gouge! Stab!

Rely on it
to unleash you.

Mourn there
what you cannot speak.

Grieve there
those illusions

you never imagined
you would have to lose.

Home From The Writer's Conference

It takes time to travel
between the world she left
and the world she returns to
where words mean only what they say
and things really are what they seem.
Somewhere back home again
she picks up the dish towel,
crushes it against her mouth.

This May Have All Been Said Before, But

don't you think
those trees
on that slope
look rather like
elderly aunts

whose lives and
contributions
have slowed
considerably,
whose feast days

have thinned
over the years,
as friends pass on,
but who still don
a new hat

come Easter,
new garden gloves
come spring,
and because
it's hard

to travel
so far or at all
send a fine
fall mum for
Thanksgiving?

Building Fence

They eyeballed the slope, the old fencer
and my friend, trued up the line, had good tools,
knew what they were doing; I doubted I could
dig one post hole for them, grabbed out small bits
of soil and what they called rotten rock,
careful to pace myself so I would last.

Sections of new fencing ran down the slope
like large basting stitches, inspiring me
to start another hole, but soon my spade sparked on stone
and I groaned, "How big do you suppose this rock is?"
The old fencer only grunted and said,
"You'll know when you get it out of there."

Several times he had us sit on warped railings
so he could nail them straight, and it was fine
from up on those good bleacher seats
when the horses streamed past, snorting and squealing,
a regular show it was, with the killdeer
fluttering and squawking before the dogs.

Then with his crowbar he hunkered down
before my hole to loosen more gravel for me.
"Can't buy holes, but folks can steal them,"
he twinkled, and glad to be resting again,
I told him what the farmer said when he found
three deep holes in his yard: "Well, well, well!"

When I took another breather to philosophize,
"You know this project would make a good poem,"
my friend cracked, "She always has been into analysis,
not action!" She was right. I probably was helping out
purely to write this poem. I'd figured out early on
it was easier to write about barn building
than build one.

The Pruning Poem

I like pruning
Clipping bushes
Shaping shrubs
Cutting offending branches
That crisscross or rub

Removing vertical ones
Where I envision
An umbrella shape
Or a curved shoot
To encourage linear spears

When I take out
What is there
I make a shape as surely
As the artist drawing lines
Or spreading colors

While pruning I must see
As the sculptor does
Chipping away at marble
Revealing the shoulder
The slender throat

Now some force
Beyond my control
Is pruning my life too
Taking some people out
Leaving others in

Ezequiel At Six

When we saw tall cornfields brown and dry,
rustling and ready for cutting, we pulled over
to the side of a road, and ventured on foot

into dappled corridors of corn, widened some places
into rooms, where stalks had failed to thrive,
or deer had browsed seedlings clean.

We felt how hard it was to walk
across the rows, how easy going straight,
making every now and then a one row jog

deeper into the field. "We could be
trapped in here if we don't watch out," the boy
half-warned me, half-hoped. "We could go

so far we couldn't hear cars on the road,
or see any landmarks, or read the sun.
And when stars came out, we couldn't read them either."

Gladly my imagination took up the thread of his tale:
And all night passing through fields we would hear
other creatures who love corn too, raccoon and deer,

wrestling with the rustling corn, always wary
of coyote or skunk or fox, those who shrink
before the moon's bright beacon.

We'd walk the whispering corn, brushing away
grasshoppers, until we were too tired
to go further, when, mysteriously,

some aura from a rise in the ground
would beckon us enter the rock-strewn mouth
of a hidden cave, where we could rest until day.

When Ezequiel Was Eight

he came to visit us in wintertime, and though he came
empty-handed, he left me an artistic array of presents.

Gold magic marker flecks suddenly adorned my desk
and an intaglio of ink x's bordered my mouse pad.

Scissor snips of paper decorated the hall rug,
and what did I find on the teak end table? Ink etchings!

Undoubtedly formed from a broken ball point pen into shapes
more artistic than accidental, but unfortunately, indelible.

Picture hooks and nails impaled our rubber wine corks,
twisting them into totems of gargoyles, forever porous.

Paper clips linked into chains soon draped the chandelier
and candlesticks displayed a new set of hieroglyphics,

their wax shavings on the high gloss table mounded about them
into a miniature village of tepees set amidst mountains.

Shish-kebab skewers glued with feathers had nose-dived
like arrows through the den into plush leather targets,

or lashed together with masking tape, sailed down
basement stairs to quiver forever in the mesh fireplace screen.

He showed me that my arrangement of paper whites now drooping
from the buffet really looked a lot like an alien's face,

pointed out its leafy crevice mouth, its multiple, bulging eyes.
Perhaps it was that alien who had festooned our frosty storm door

with ornate scrollings from some indeterminate alphabet.
Surely, we both agreed, it was the work of someone from another planet!

July Fourth

On the horizon off toward Middleton and Verona
fireworks burst silent showers against the sky

so she wrapped a sleeping bag around her fiddle,
and went out to the barn to watch from the new hay.

The full moon was as low as the ramp to the loft,
and she sat in the wide door, watching it glow

like a celestial campfire. Unwrapping her fiddle
she played western tunes until a muffled shuffling

told her horses were processing up from the lower field
encircling the ramp, evenly spaced, heads lowered

like communicants, listening.

Mood Indigo

When he heard his father had died,
His shoulders slumped —
He marched straight from phone to piano
To take up with a vengeance the Rogers and Hart
The old man had played: *Manhattan,*
Thou Swell, Blue Room,
You Took Advantage Of Me.

Next he polished up songs from his own teens,
Bewitched, Bothered and Bewildered,
Misty, Mood Indigo, Spring Is Here,
Sensing only vaguely his depression.

Now he comforts himself at the piano
Trying out new voicings and chords
For golden oldies he loves.
From out in the spring garden
His wife hears him tear into
I Get A Kick Out of You;
Into her kitchen come strains of
My Heart Stood Still, and
Someone To Watch Over Me.

To An Old Piano

Praise my piano's physical beauty, its curves
and finish and gleam. Sing its sleek smoothness
and sturdy sides which embrace me when I seat myself

before it, enjoying the striking pattern of black against
white. Praise its shining pedals, so comfortable

underfoot, which I have had repaired so they will not squeak
as they sustain the tone. Praise how it fills this room with
its presence as it did my childhood home, providing challenge,

solace and satisfaction as I practiced, or did not practice, but
dreamed or trembled, head hidden against fluttering sheet music.

Praise its shining surface, sometimes covered against
late summer sun, sometimes exposed and graced with sculpture
or a striking vase of delphinium. Praise its matching

bench with hinged lid which holds my music and sometimes
hidden Easter eggs. Praise the brass lamp which bends
to focus brightness on the page, and the three hymnals

which taught me to sight read. Praise the keys which
do not click, the strings which do not twang, the marvelous

old sounding board which is not cracked, and the soft new felts
which temper the sound to the size of this particular room.

In short, I speak against selling this heirloom to remodel
the kitchen. I decry progress and digital pianos.
I speak for this piano, as it has spoken for me.

Let's Say I Still Have The Slightest Trickle Of Poetry Left In Me

Will I allow it to be engulfed
by torrents of CNN news

or deluged by a rising tide
of televised NCAA games

before March Madness whirls in
when it most surely will drown

(if confounding technology
hasn't already killed it)

or will I protect, even deepen
its creek bed, clearing off

entangled embankments
rolling away boulders

that hesitant waters
may flow along lightly

sparkling in sunlight
to join stronger streams?

IN MY TIME

In My Time

I have searched for special things gone lost somehow,
an heirloom bracelet on a woodland trail,
jade beads in a snow bank, pearls in dark pools,

not to mention trifles such as car keys,
a contact lens or earring, which everyone
knows renders the remaining one useless,

favorite things grown so familiar
I thoughtlessly wore them to wild places
where I blend myself with what I love.

I've searched for special dogs gone lost somehow,
distracted by deer, scent, or a covey
of tireless children playing fetch the stick,

dogs disoriented by firework shows,
trapped in culverts or turned loose in new towns.
I've called their names from hills into valleys,

driven country roads slowly at first light.
I've shouted myself hoarse in quiet streets
to find the scrappy dogs I loved.

I've searched for many things gone lost somehow,
but you – you are gone, not lost, but missing,
hidden, and I am not allowed to search for you,

must not write, email, or phone anyone
connected to you, pumping them for leads.
I can't find you by offering rewards,

or tramping deep ravines. So I walk the pine paths
you would remember, and want you to know
that from one continent to another,

I am calling your name.

Embracing Herself

She awakes hugging herself until it hurts. A contortionist
could not hold a position more tightly. Surely this embrace
is meant to comfort, not detain. Breathless, she does not
realize how hard she clutches until her shoulders ache and
numb along their contours. She has dreamed of long low
hills at twilight, one serpentine road, untraveled, disappearing
deep into the horizon, going who knew how far or where.
But at any beginning doesn't someone offer
the arm slung across the shoulder, the good luck pat
on the back? She holds herself harder, hoping to calm
the scurrying in her chest.

Caterpillars Who Turn and Turn

Caterpillars who turn and turn
inside their cocoons
have nothing on me.
Nights I wear nightgowns
are hardest to unravel.
Tossing from left to front,
to right to back, spinning always
in the same direction,
its length tightens upon me
like a shroud or swaddling,
swaddling or shroud
no power, not even sleep, can unwind.
But what I want to know is
after such turbulent gestation,
what will struggle forth
and be born?

Twice Shy

If when she leaves she looks back in the mirror
and sees her mother crying at the curb
but keeps her foot off the brake, presses steadily
on toward the big city, the better job

and if sometimes at night she lies awake
sobbing, because no one, not even mother's
little girl can have it all, the old home
and a new self, does she decide right then

how it must be for her, she would find solace
in writing and a ministry of friends,
not in daughters, who from their first breath on
must be forced out from her to live away

even though she had spent her days preparing
the rich matrix of love which helped them leave?

At The Cove

Beyond reach of adult shouts
beyond water fights
and cries to "watch me!"
Beyond pail and shovel squabbles,
spilled soda pop and kicked sand,
the breakwater rocks
formed our secluded cove.
We lowered our straps
and sometimes our suits,
fitting limbs over rocks
as easily as snakes,
letting our hips
tell us, this is rock,
this throne, centuries
of pressed sand,
seeing through drowsy lashes
against our upper arms
barges disappearing
beyond the pencil-thin
horizon.

Our daily mutiny,
to seek the cove's seclusion,
the lake swell's embrace.
Pressed against warm rocks
we eluded sharp winds
and the abandoned adults
who tried to reel us in.
That summer between earth and lake
the reef was ours alone.
Undulating wide and deep,
furrows slid softly between
pilings, nudging the rocks,
sending up plumes of spray
to moisten our taut skin.
Billows beckoned to us

Come slide in,
come rise and fall
in the arching
in the scrolling sea.

We saw submerged rocks
descending
like George Braque's steps
and had enough sense
not to dive.
But we could leap
head up, legs spread,
the jump lifeguards use
to keep their goal in sight,
and then it was just us,
naked and free
beyond the pilings.

Later, ascending
through mossy grottos,
we felt purified,
tied garlands from kelp
for our necks, for our hair.
Drying fast, we absorbed
the heat of one rock surface,
then inched on to a fresh baking spot,
leaving behind us on the rocks
the damp carapace
of our changing selves.

Leaving Home

My car is nosed into the garage
like a boat tied in a slip,
the driveway my channel to open sea.
They are royalty, waving already.
I try to back away straight, and fail.
My rear wheels touch grass –
No clean getaway for me.
I must go forward to leave again.
More bowing and scraping.
I whip the wheel around,
arms tense, palms sweating.
This happens whenever I leave,
the false starts,
the heading back home
to get straightened out.
At last I stay on the straight and narrow
all the way out to the road.
Finally I can shift out of reverse.
If I weren't forty, I'd floor it.

Villanelle for Dropouts at 8:30 a.m.

Anyone with a place to go is already there.
At school or at home, they doubt they'll be missed.
They say they don't hurt when they can't say where.

More than most, they must know the world's not fair.
But then, who needs feelings or jobs, to exist?
Anyone with a place to go is already there.

Feeling good about oneself is as rare
As an eclipse; hiding from goals they don't dare risk,
They say they don't hurt when they can't say where.

With what flair they insist they just don't care,
Hang out on corners, dream of girls they might kiss,
But anyone with a place to go is already there.

There's nothing on earth they say they won't dare.
I know of no fiction sadder than this:
They say they don't hurt when they can't say where.

The farther they drop, the harder to share;
There's little adults say they won't resist.
Anyone with a place to go is already there.
They say they don't hurt when they can't say where.

You Sleep So Lightly

You sleep so lightly
beneath the quilt I sewed
I can scarcely see your outline,
must pat my hand along the puff
as one gropes along the wall
in the night for the switch.

Though you are already asleep
I tuck you in, outlining your body.
Lying straight and on your back
you seem a mummy, a child Pharaoh,
your pale hair radiating across the pillow
like an ancient headdress of the sun.

With you nightly, I will not notice
how your shape gradually thickens and lengthens,
putting that much more matter between us.
One night when I bend down to kiss you,
I will be surprised to find
your tiny transparent face is changed,
is inscrutable as a stone carving.
Though you are not dead,
that night I will cry.

From The Other Room

What I wanted to say was:

Let me hold you to sleep
close in this burrow
batten our ears
against distant storms

Let's circle three times
to soften our bed
and breathe each other's dreams
unfurrowed by fears.

Let me close your lids
with lips as soft
as the moth fluttering
now against the light.

What I said was:

Goodnight.

Through A Glass Darkly

Standing by the light switch
brushing my hair in the almost dark
I nevertheless face the wall
where the mirror hangs
pretending
I want to see
as when I read psychology
I seem to want to know
what I would rather die
than change.

Who would doubt I bought
that first horse for her?
Question wanting her to have
the finest instruments and teachers?
And if at times I seemed harsh
who would guess I was scouring
my own rank faults
while saying I did so
for her own good?

I suppose I will continue
consulting obscure mirrors
making now and then
deft but minor adjustments
with my hair or skin
knowing better than most
how trying it is
to square what one knows
with what one does.

Just now
when she wrenched free
from a love as traditional and secure
as high mass
all day I told myself
I was crying
for her.

Whose Show Is It, Anyway?

You're cast, kid,
you've got the script,
you've got technique,
you've learned to improvise.
Somewhere along the way
you picked up a sense of timing,
some pretty special effects.
You know what you want
and how to go for it.
I'm just the producer
who set this whole thing in motion –
you build the character.
So why do I sit here
at the back of the hall
calling "Cut! Cut!"
waving my hands wildly
in the dark?

My Sister The Archivist
Inspects Family Snapshots

I wonder where it went, this sparse painting
I see here behind Dad. Some northern hillside,
brown and bronze trunks, weren't they?
Against gray snow? What could have happened to it?
I wonder why it isn't here with their other fine art. . .

I'd hate to tell you about that painting.
It was a painting so bleak I felt cold standing near it.
It spoke of no landscape I had ever known
or cherished, nor could I understand who would,
or why, for so long, it had claimed pride of place
in our childhood home. So when I needed a large frame
for some gift shop print or other
when our children were small, I simply pried
the thing loose and crushed it into the trash
without a moment's remorse, never thinking
to return it to dad, or save it myself,
or put it out to consignment, so sure I was
no one would want what I did not.

And this rug with the roses near Mother's bed here,
It's so fine, could it have been hooked of silk?
I remember that rug, I'm sure I do.
It was in the guest room of our first house,
and Grandma slept there, and we did too,
when we were sick. I remember taking my slippers off
to feel its cool. Wasn't the wallpaper all roses too?
And didn't she say we three were her real and true American
Beauties? Whatever happened to that rug?
It must be worth a fortune now, don't you suppose?

I'd hate to tell you about that rug. I liked it too,
and asked mother for it one day when I saw it
in her laundry room, on the cement floor, and
quite dirty it was too. Couldn't we have it cleaned?
I asked her, but she said no, it would cost a fortune,
it wasn't worth it, so I tried to wash it myself
and when I did, it came out in tatters;
alas, how one cleans things really matters.

Oh! Here's one of Dad's workbench!
He had so little time to putter, poor man, but look
at all these old tools he had saved from somewhere.
And these double runner skates and sleigh bells,
don't they speak of another time and place?
I know you display them out at the cabin,
but look at that coffee grinder and smoothing iron!
I wonder whatever happened to them?

Oh those domestic treasures! I can't bear to tell you.
Our backdoor neighbor on Joss Court
took quite a shine to them, remembered her own mother
using something like them when she was a girl,
said she'd be thrilled to have them. So I gave them to her
instead of to the church resale that spring. Dust catchers!
that's what I thought they were then, and always wondered
why some folks set such great store by them.

I Wish For My Own Bring-Far-Near-Glass

because we move, you and I, as if under water,
blurred with day dreams and with sleep,
calling to each other across great distances,
our messages aborted because we do not listen.

But at tonight's musical I marveled to see
a man I know was deaf from birth avidly
watch his son sign for him the songs they came
to hear his grandson sing.

And think how long the prodigal's father
must have been watching for his son's return
for it says it was *from afar* that he first glimpsed
his son on the horizon, returning home

and it is *from afar* that the Inuit's wife scans the snow
with their ancient bring-far-near-glass
reading the message her husband paces out for her
to the right, then to the left of his dog sled

as clearly as if it were black script against the snow
so that she understands he has with him a guest
and rises to thaw a third piece of fish
near their brass oil lamp.

Run My Good Sheep, Run

Remember, in the dusk, after dinner,
in dusty spots, on cool cement sidewalks
or on lawns where the sprinklers didn't reach
how we would play our block games, Kick the Can,
Round the Moon, Run My Good Sheep, Run?
I hated being *it*. What if I couldn't catch anyone?

The older kids hated me even more
for the way I played, said it was no fair
guarding goal so close they couldn't run home free.
They said it was no fun never being searched for.
I knew that myself all along.
Who doesn't want to be found

waiting in the long grasses until the steps
come nearer, even making little sounds
to give yourself away, until you are spotted,
when suddenly you don't want to be
caught at all, you want to be in safe and free,
screaming and sprinting towards home.

Sometimes I like to think you're out there now
in the dust and long grasses, waiting to be found,
but I keep on playing our game the old childish way;
I'm still cautious and cheat. I will be here,
still hovering around goal, when you give up
and don't want to hide anymore.

CULTIVATING BLUEBIRDS

All Around Me, This Coming and Going, This Breaking And Mending

I sit at the counter near the window mending with ceramic glue
a favorite bowl. A robin swoops in under the eave above me to
the nest she has fastened with her own kind of glue to the crook
in the drainpipe. I have seen her flashing shadow all spring.
Her first brood fell prey to a vagrant cat and a battalion of crows
before the terrible ruckus alerted me to their plight. Now again
she feeds four fledglings, then darts off for another fat white
grub, each time carrying away debris from the nest. Standing
on its rim, her young try out their wings as they watch her fly.
They will be gone by tomorrow.

A highly vocal house wren conducts a tour of possible sites
he has prepared for his mate's nesting pleasure. I hung three
houses this year, hoping they would choose one, and know from
watching that they have been well lined. Three fighting fish,
magnified by the curvature of their wide mouthed glass bowl,
evaluate my patience with this gluing project from their position
atop a small television. Twice, startled by the sudden rustle of
dropped grocery bags, the biggest fish has hurtled himself out
of the bowl to the floor, but been rescued in time. Now I protect
him with a fine mesh spatter guard borrowed from the stove.

Piece by jagged piece I work to reassemble the beautiful bowl,
guided by grooves which created an intricate swirling pattern I
hope will conceal my clumsy reconstruction. Pressing together
the pieces, I become an instrument, I am the vise. How slowly
the glue seems to dry, with only my fingers attempting to establish
the cant and slant the potter first whirled at her wheel. Outside
the window I see the trailing begonias beginning to cascade
satisfactorily along with repotted English ivy, and just beyond
them, much earlier than last year, a large planting of rocket
flowers is sending up its yellow spires. Pup gives up hoping for
a walk, positions himself strategically between me and the door
for a nap. On his tummy, paws tucked under, he looks like the
autumn wooly caterpillars I watched on sidewalks as a child. I
sit still too, holding on.

Disclaimer

I don't mind, I'm not sad, when goldenrod
Unfurls its gilded spray, when sumac flourishes
Its first flags beneath succulent
Spires, or when elderberry's rich black
Trumps milkweed, thistle.

It doesn't bother me at all to find
Half shell fungus ledges climbing mossy
Tree trunks like steps, or puff balls glowing bright
Against leaves in dappled light.

I like to see Indian peace pipes clustering
In tiny conspiracies between roots of trees
Where collected rain water waits to slake
The dog's thirst, or ground bees toil to fill hives
With nectar gleaned from ripe apples, wild plums.

These days I watch the moon rise earlier,
See grasses flower and dry, feel autumn
Approach on cool morning winds
As a new crop of children traipse to kindergarten
And I take a light jacket just in case
When heading out to ride with nary
A thought about which state is better,
The time of the blossom or the time of the berry.

On Disappearing Cloaks

"The cloaks we had wrapped about our
essential selves were wearing thin"

Robertson Davies

If growing old means showing more and more
of our essential selves, let me hasten the process!
Let me find the rip cord, and the courage to use it!

Let me unravel all ruse, all hypocrisy
by which we keep others from knowing us
and us from knowing ourselves.

Let the nap be worn away, let the patterns emerge,
etched and luminescent, like flowers
in a prized Persian carpet.

Let the cloak become, not shabby, but transparent.
Let our spirits glow, let everyone know
that what they see is what in fact we are.

To My Mother In Her Grave—
Don't Worry! Now I *AM* Just Like You!

Now I make my bed first thing
Close every cupboard door each time
And never read in bad light

Turn off un-needed overheads
Lock the doors when I leave
And wear socks to bed

Rise first to pour juice and cereal
And pull yesterday's shoes
From under the dining room table

Have a cleaning lady at last
A place for purse and pills
And am never without my umbrella

Have a garage door opener
An electric key for the car
A drink with the news before dinner

Attend three reading/writing groups
Two theater series, one concert series
And sometimes the opera

Summer in the east
Winter in the southwest
Or cruise the South Pacific

Wash dinner dishes alone
After others drift off—
Go to bed before everyone else

Out Out

Get away, grim reaper, don't take me yet,
I am not ready for harvesting!
My knees may click, my hip joint stick,
My toes creak and hesitate on hikes,
But swing your scythe someplace else.

Or rather, don't brandish it at all.
You have done enough for one lifetime,
Hurling at close friends cataracts and cancers,
Ruptured appendices, cruel lymphomas.
I am not ready for harvesting!

Hide your grimace in your ragged sleeve,
Make your solitary way down that other lane.
Wield your blade on dead trees or fields of wheat,
Go sweep cobwebs from the night.
For heaven's sake, get a life!

Going Downhill

Dorothy is slipping, have you noticed?
She forgets the names of the commonest things,
Tells most stories twice.
I can see it.
Every week, a little bit more.
But she's not half as bad as Marion –
She's really slipped!
Sight long since gone, poor thing,
Now it's her hearing.

So have Trudi and Agnes – slipped.
I saw them at circle last week –
They both fell asleep in their chairs!
I do grow a bit tired afternoons.
But you should see Clara and Claudine,
They don't go out at all anymore.
They're just slipping,
Slip, slip, slipping away,
But I'm not, am I dear?
Slipping, that is?

These Simple Bouquets
(The Song of a Flower Maniac)

It is still too hot, but soon I am going out to pick daisies
and perennial sweetpeas and if I have time, some more shastas
to go with gallardias I see have opened, and perhaps several
sprays of floribunda, because you know how they jazz up
almost any place, and certainly a few johnny jump-ups
to mix with the ever present forget-me-nots,
a mini nosegay for a condiments tray.

After I have stood in the evening silence
arranging the long stems and the short
into various indoor oases, I will glide about,
deciding where they make the best statement
about themselves, the vase, and the room.

Then, when everyone returns, tossing books, shuffling mail,
fixing ice tea, dropping down to watch the news,
I will keep my eyes upon these simple bouquets,
believing it is their power, their beauty,
which drew the family home
and now makes possible their rest.

Early One Morning

A naming spirit wafted into my garden, hovering briefly over plants which friends have shared with me in summers past, 'starts' or 'cuttings,' they called them, of the mother plant they had tended for years in their own gardens.

To the wild orange mass I call the Louise, the imp distinctly conferred the name columbine, then sped on to my climbing Jesse, whispering over it the phrase yellow rose, and to my Marie, just attaining the fence, the name white clematis. My Isabels she dubbed primrose, to my Pauls, prairie smoke, my Lyn, lavender. Who could keep up with her? My Nancys she called bachelor buttons, my Claras soldiers buttons, my Jeans, wild ginger, my Sauls trillium and my Dorothys, a lovely word, new to me, spring anemone.

"But what about me?" chorused my stunning blue forget-me-nots to the naming spirit (or rather, "What about us?", because even they could see there were quite a lot of them. "What about us?")

You are well-named already, said the spirit, for your little faces will prompt her someday to remember that you were once grown by her father. He dug your roots up for her out of a corner of his back yard where they provided good ground cover, as you do so handsomely here, and time and again he carried many spaded clumps to Madison, all carefully wrapped in The Kenosha Evening News in the trunk of his car. And yet, though your gardener has insisted upon memorializing her friends by changing the names of their flower gifts, she has forgotten to memorialize his gift. You will know your work is finished when you hear her call you My Dads.

Sawyer Kissed Me

I held him, pushed him, bounced him,
hiked him, echoed him, admired him,
made faces for him and silly sounds,
clapped my hands and danced him round,
shook my shoulders, drummed his tray,
let him climb me, and twist away,
shared his slippery apple bites,
all to his delight. Then, last night
he inclined unto me, so that somewhere
near my face I felt his happy open mouth.

Now I may be old, and no one's grandma,
but that random bump was not hit or miss.
You may say that life has missed me,
but just remember, Sawyer kissed me!

Playing With The Sun

I played chutes and ladders, pac man too
with the new red sun today
risen two minutes fresher than before
and still so low on the horizon
I could hook it on the branches
of this tree and that like an ornament
too fragile for a child to touch.
Where the bare branches of a maple
flared like the arms of the menorah
in silhouette between us I marched
the sun up the left side of the ladder
and down the right, simply by walking myself
down and then, backwards, up, the hill.
I bounced the sun along the spires
of spruce like the moving ball in silent films
that tells people which pitch to sing.
I froze it behind a giant pine,
making an instant scissor cutting of the tree.
I rolled it along telephone wires
and lodged it in chimney pots
like a great golden egg of Amsterdam.

But there came a time when no matter
how fast I walked backwards up the hill,
I could not batten it down anymore,
and the yellowing sun wafted gently
upwards, and away, like a balloon
whose child has let go the string.

Cultivating Bluebirds

If I start talking bluebirds, you're going to get all hung up
on happiness, think I'm noticing how quietly it comes,
how swiftly it flies away, but from riding, I see that some folk
do cultivate bluebirds, place specially crafted houses
around open glades or meadows, check them periodically
to clean out old nests, count eggs or hatchlings,
repair their boxes from the ravages of rascally raccoons.

As a matter of fact, maybe I **am** talking about happiness,
because this summer I have seen two nests,
one of them toward the top of an old-fashioned
wooden fence post, not a man-made birdhouse,
but a hollowed-out spot in a rotten post,
the other nest knocked tipsy on its metal pole
as if some marauder, that raccoon again,
or a huge crow, had wrenched it awry in landing.
We laughed at its crazy tilt as we rode up to it,
it did look drunken amidst all the other houses
aligned on their poles straight as soldiers,
marching along the weed-entangled way,

laughed until we came abreast its lop-sided entrance
and saw a small feathery face peering out at us,
waiting for lunch I suppose, not a troupe of riders
stunned to a stop, all laughter stifled by seeing such brave expectations
in one so small in so precarious a dwelling in such a terrible world.

And yes I can tell you it did make me glad, even happy
to know he can survive there against all odds, may even thrive
to raise other fledglings who will swoop out into the meadow
among the sailing butterflies and darting dragon flies,
settling sometimes, however clumsily, upon the nodding goldenrod.

Lullaby of Solar Lights

All day the enormous sun
fuels our garden lamps
which hoard sunbeams
until daylight ends
and even the glommen
fades into darkness.

Oh then the tiny lamps
expend their treasure
as night calls forth soft
beacons from stony niches
or clumps of pale fall
flowering anemone.

And how long their glow
burns star-like holes
in night's black cloak
only owls know.

Snow Everywhere Descending

Folded in repose
my hands startle me

large knuckles
blue veins, crepy skin

yet they rest in each other
like good friends.

When I cross them
to grasp my upper arms

I have a fine basket
woven of me

a simple hollow
to cradle my head.

The Heartbreak Of A Half Step

Who has not felt the heartbreak of a half step?
It catches at the throat.
Music dwells in the intervals,
Not in the lonely notes on either side.
How far the spaces are, in pitch and in time,
Creates the meaning, makes the mood.
So though you are a man of science
While I am immersed in words
Doesn't matter half as much
As the song that sings between us.

Rural Woman Killed By Tree

They made the place run, even if it
didn't exactly hum those last few years
when one crop was all the hay they'd cut
and left machinery standing out in the field
far into fall. And so it stood the day
we all went tearing up there to pry her
free from the aspen tree he felled on her,
worrying as the cutter always does, saying
"Stand back now, Ma! Don't come too close!"
But she was always one to be in the thick of things,
thinking she knew best and wanting to help.
So there she lay, her pelvis crushed, the brush
from the fallen tree arching above her head,
the leaves like laminated petals shimmering lightly
against that blue of an October sky.

For a long time we asked ourselves why
the boy didn't use the saw to free her himself
instead of rushing down to town for help,
help that had to be a long time coming
to one waiting crushed among dried grass and leaves
for something to unfasten her and set her free.
But he never could get a job done right.
They laid her to rest in late afternoon
some two days later, and a few of us were told
how the sun filled that church and made its floors
of hardwood maple glow like streets of gold.

In The Fullness Of Time

Oh incremental slowness,
I love watching you spread
green dotted lines
over winter plowed fields!
I love watching you creep
a brilliant yellow up ragwort spires,
and bulge tight knots of hydrangea
into creamy, billowing blooms.

In your time, in your time,
the vine lengthens and twines,
the Labrador violet curls
farther along rocky cracks.
I see Irish moss sending forth
its stars, feathered grasses
unfurling their plumes,
milkweed pods swelling with silk.

Oh slow steady force
unfolding the world,
you have blessed me
and given me peace.

You Let Me Be

You let me be as I was meant to be,
not pruned to please a parent's sense of right.
Is that what it is about you, for me,

this permission to let my senses flow free
without fear of abandonment some dark night?
You remind me of how I was meant to be

'til shades of the prison house damped memory
of sand dunes, and songs round campfires bright.
Is that what it is about you, for me,

a brush with my past, kindling unerringly
feelings others often repress from sight?
When you let me be as I was meant to be

I became more than I was, gracefully
able to love myself, cease my desperate flight.
So that's what it is about you, for me!

Now pulsations of pain change to sympathy,
and you who behold the world with delight,
you let me be as I was meant to be—
that's what it is about you, for me.

Three Jolly Horsemen Went Out
For A Ride One Night

A new moon hung above the tree fringe
like an orange slipper so we chose trails
where we continued to see it against the darkening sky

but when we emerged into a long unmowed meadow
what we came upon were fireflies, millions of them,
a shower of orange entities spilled from the moon's shoe.

Scientists I asked called it their aggregation display,
an orgy of delegates convened in sexual congress.
But I like to think that shower of sparks came from Thor himself,

striking his mighty hammer on the immense anvil of the earth,
bedecking with one blow the spiking blue stem before us.
And because the plain field now emitted the kind of holy light

artists show arising from mangers, or preceding angels at annunciations,
we reined in abruptly and stared at the transformed land so long
the afterimages streaked and blurred like flashing comets.

Finally, because the horses chewed their bits and pawed, we plunged,
as if diving into a glinting coral sea, into the ignited meadow where
fireflies lit upon the horse's bridle bands and ear tips like jewels,

tangled in their swishing tails, and flashed around their fetlocks,
eventually adorning our own hair and heels as we parted the long grasses,
electric horsemen now, elevating into a star studded night.

About the Author

Karen Updike lives and writes in Madison, Wisconsin. She taught high school English and later creative writing to older adults. She has an earlier Fireweed chapbook, Off Riding, and has co-authored a book, Writers Have No Age published by The Haworth Press.